D0518551

CRICKET

Wit

CRICKET WIT

First published as WICKET WIT in 2006
Reprinted 2006, 2007, 2008, 2009, 2011
This edition copyright © Summersdale Publishers Ltd, 2013

Illustrations © Alan Gilliland Graphics

Summersdale Publishers Ltd
46 West Street
Chichester
West Sussex
PO19 1RP
UK

www.summersdale.com

Printed and bound by CPI Group (UK) Ltd, Croydon, CR0 4YY

ISBN: 978-1-84953-462-8

Substantial discounts on bulk quantities of Summersdale books are available to corporations, professional associations and other organisations. For details contact Nicky Douglas by telephone: +44 (0) 1243 756902, fax: +44 (0) 1243 786300 or email: nicky@summersdale.com.

CRICKET

Wit

QUIPS AND QUOTES FOR THE CRICKET-OBSESSED

RICHARD BENSON

summersdale

CONTENTS

CONTENTS

EDITOR'S NOTE

HRH the Duke of Edinburgh once scoffed at the 'widely held and quite erroneous belief that cricket is just another game'. This eclectic compendium, for its part, ably disproves such misconceptions, showing how the relevance of cricket extends beyond the pitch to literature, society, politics and philosophy. In fact, the gentleman's game has inspired some of the most profound insights and off-the-cuff humour to be found in any collection of quotations.

Amongst these pages there are timeless classics as well as a few more obscure commentaries to raise the eyebrow of even the most dedicated cricket fanatic. From cricketers to commentators, celebrities to politicians, poets to comedians, it seems everyone has something to say about this age-old game. There's banter about the pitfalls of batting and bowling, quirky quips about the nuances of the game and acidic attacks from and on the press. Dip into each section and you are sure to find something to crease you up.

The delightful mix of run-out rebuttals, wicket wisecracks, oval orations and howzat humiliations in this side-splitting book will ensure you'll never be stumped for a return again.

BATTING

David Gower makes
batting look as easy
as drinking tea.

LEONARD HUTTON, ENGLISH CRICKETER

It's hard work making
batting look effortless.

DAVID GOWER, ENGLISH TELEVISION
PERSONALITY AND CRICKETER

———•●•———

Cricket is a batsman's game.
The city of London has never
emptied to watch a bowler as
it did to watch Bradman.

E. W. SWANTON, ENGLISH CRICKET WRITER AND COMMENTATOR

———•●•———

I couldn't bat for the length
of time required to score 500.
I'd get bored and fall over.

DENIS COMPTON, ENGLISH CRICKETER

When I was watching
Fred Astaire I used to think,
here was a chap who would
have been a great batsman.

LEONARD HUTTON

Whenever I saw Wally Hammond
batting, I felt sorry for the ball.

LEONARD HUTTON

When you win the toss – bat.
If you are in doubt, think
about it, then bat. If you
have very big doubts, consult
a colleague – then bat.

W. G. GRACE, ENGLISH CRICKETER AND DOCTOR

–●●–

When I'm batting, I like to
pretend I'm a West Indian.

DARREN GOUGH, ENGLISH CRICKETER

He looks like and bats like a librarian: a prodder, a nudger, with a virile bottom hand that works the ball to the on side, and a top hand for keeping his other glove on.

MIKE SELVEY, ENGLISH CRICKET CORRESPONDENT AND CRICKETER, ON BERT VANCE'S TEST DEBUT

I never wanted to make a hundred. Who wants to make a hundred anyway? When I first went in, my immediate objective was to hit the ball to each of the four corners of the field. After that, I tried not to be repetitive.

LORD LEARIE CONSTANTINE, TRINIDADIAN CRICKETER AND POLITICAL ACTIVIST

They came to see
me bat, not to
see you bowl.

W. G. GRACE ON REFUSING TO LEAVE THE CREASE
HAVING BEEN BOWLED OUT BY THE FIRST BALL

BOWLING

I don't want to do
the batsman any
permanent injury, just
to cause him concern
– to hurt him a bit.

DENNIS LILLEE, AUSTRALIAN CRICKETER

You can't buy one of them
at a local superstore – it
takes years and years.

DARREN GOUGH ON A GOOD ONE-DAY BOWLER

———— ••• ————

I bowl so slow that if after I
have delivered the ball I don't
like the look of it, I can run
after it and bring it back.

J. M. BARRIE, SCOTTISH NOVELIST AND DRAMATIST

To be a great fast
bowler, you need
a big heart and
a big bottom.

FRED TRUEMAN, ENGLISH COMMENTATOR,
AUTHOR AND CRICKETER

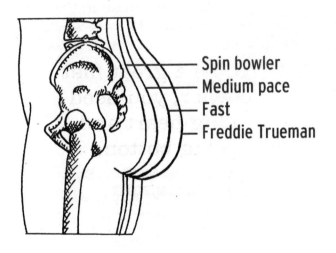

Spin bowler
Medium pace
Fast
Freddie Trueman

I try to hit the batsman in the ribcage when I bowl a purposeful bouncer, and I want it to hurt so much that the batsman doesn't want to face me anymore.

DENNIS LILLEE

You must treat a cricket ball like a new bride.

MICKY STEWART, ENGLISH CRICKETER AND ENGLAND CRICKET MANAGER

He bowls like an
octopus with piles.

UNKNOWN AUSTRALIAN ON ENGLISH CRICKETER DEREK
RANDALL, AS REPORTED BY MATTHEW ENGEL

———•••———

I was once timed at
99.97 mph, but that's rubbish –
I was miles faster than that.

JEFF THOMPSON, AUSTRALIAN BOWLER,
REPUTED TO BE THE FASTEST EVER

———•••———

His bowling is like shooting down
F-16s with sling shots. Even if
they hit, no damage would be done.

COLIN CROFT, WEST INDIES CRICKETER, ON
ANGUS FRASER IN THE GUYANA TEST

Fast bowling isn't hard
work, it's horse work.

FRED TRUEMAN

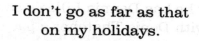

I don't go as far as that
on my holidays.

UNKNOWN BOWLER, COMMENTING ON THE
LENGTH OF BOB WILLIS'S RUN-UP

There's nothing wrong with
being aggressive – the bloke
down the other end has a bat,
some pads and a helmet.

SIMON JONES, WELSH CRICKETER

Cowans should remember what happened to Graham Dilley, who started out as a genuinely quick bowler. They started stuffing 'line and length' into his ear, and now he has Dennis Lillee's action with Denis Thatcher's pace.

GEOFF BOYCOTT, ENGLISH COMMENTATOR AND CRICKETER

———•••———

Though essentially good-natured, he had that vital weapon in the fast bowler's armoury: grumpiness.

SIMON HUGHES, ENGLISH JOURNALIST, AUTHOR AND CRICKETER, ON ANGUS FRASER

CELEBRITIES ON CRICKET

I am confident they
play cricket in heaven.
Wouldn't be heaven
otherwise, would it?

PATRICK MOORE, ASTRONOMER

Cricket is basically
baseball on Valium.

ROBIN WILLIAMS, AMERICAN ACTOR AND COMEDIAN

Is there any sex in it?

PETER SELLERS, ENGLISH COMEDIAN AND ACTOR,
AS A PSYCHIATRIST UPON FIRST LEARNING ABOUT
CRICKET IN *WHAT'S NEW PUSSYCAT?*

Cricket is like sex films. They
relieve frustration and tension.

LINDA LOVELACE, AMERICAN ACTRESS
AND STAR OF *DEEP THROAT*

It's a funny kind
of month, October.
For the really keen
cricket fan, it's when
you realise that your
wife left you in May.

DENIS NORDEN, ENGLISH COMEDY WRITER
AND TELEVISION PRESENTER

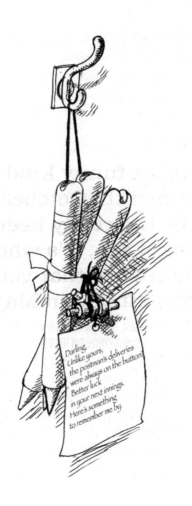

Darling,
Unlike yours,
the postman's deliveries
were always on the button.
Better luck
in your next innings.
Here's something
to remember me by.

Cricket is the only game
where you can actually put
on weight while playing.

TOMMY DOCHERTY, SCOTTISH FOOTBALLER

———— •●• ————

Nothing yet devised by man is
worse for a sick hangover than a
day's cricket in the summer sun.

MICHAEL PARKINSON, ENGLISH JOURNALIST
AND TELEVISION PRESENTER

———— •●• ————

It would be extremely difficult
for me to choose between
singing Elvis Presley songs
and scoring a century for
England, but I think I would
choose a century for England.

TIM RICE, ENGLISH LYRICIST, RADIO PRESENTER AND AUTHOR

I want to play cricket; it doesn't seem to matter if you win or lose.

MEAT LOAF, AMERICAN SINGER

———•●•———

Are you aware, Sir, that the last time I saw anything like that on a top lip, the whole herd had to be destroyed?

ERIC MORECAMBE, ENGLISH COMEDIAN, TO THE MOUSTACHIOED DENNIS LILLEE

———•●•———

When's the game itself going to begin?

GROUCHO MARX, AMERICAN COMEDIAN AND ACTOR, WHILST WATCHING A CRICKET MATCH AT LORD'S

29

Cricket needs brightening
up a bit. My solution is to let
players drink at the beginning
of the game, not after. It always
works in our picnic matches.

PAUL HOGAN, AUSTRALIAN ACTOR AND COMEDIAN

—— ●◆● ——

I find it beautiful to watch
and I like that they break
for tea. That is very cool.

JIM JARMUSCH, AMERICAN FILM DIRECTOR

There is a widely held and quite erroneous belief that cricket is just another game.

HRH THE DUKE OF EDINBURGH

———•••———

It's been a reasonable day for us boozers up here in the private boxes, but what about the geezers queuing and those blokes munching their sandwiches up there at the Nursery End?

MICK JAGGER, ENGLISH ROCK MUSICIAN, AFTER PLAY WAS ABANDONED IN THE CENTENARY TEST BETWEEN ENGLAND AND AUSTRALIA AT LORD'S

I suppose doing a love scene
with Raquel Welch roughly
corresponds to scoring a
century before lunch.

OLIVER REED, ENGLISH ACTOR

•••

I have often thought how much
better a life I would have had, what
a better man I would have been,
how much healthier an existence
I would have led, if I had been a
cricketer instead of an actor.

LAURENCE OLIVIER, ENGLISH ACTOR

CHARACTER IN CRICKET

Concentration is
sometimes mistaken
for grumpiness.

MICHAEL ATHERTON, ENGLISH JOURNALIST AND CRICKETER

Indomitable; there can be
no other epithet to sum up
the cricketing spirit in that
small and fragile frame.

DENIS MACKAIL, ENGLISH WRITER, ON J. M. BARRIE

— ● ● —

It seems that neutral umpires
were not used until about 1836
and, hitherto, provided the
umpire was a gentleman of good
repute, no objection would be
taken to his having placed a bet
on his team. It would be a point
of honour with him to carry
out his duties impartially.

GORDON ROSS, ENGLISH CRICKET JOURNALIST

Hambledon is a place that I have a strong dislike to – on account of its morals and dissipation.

GILBERT WHITE, ENGLISH NATURALIST AND ORNITHOLOGIST, IN A LETTER TO HIS BROTHER REVD JOHN WHITE, ON HAMBLEDON, WHICH AT THE TIME WAS ONE OF THE CENTRES OF CRICKET

•••

The modern cricketer is not an ogre, nor is he deliberately obstructive. Although in most cases it would be unfair to dismiss him as a spoiled brat, he is too often lazy, ill-disciplined and reluctant to put in the effort and dedication commensurate with the wages he is earning. He has a very low boredom threshold with a constant need to be told what to do with his time.

BOB WILLIS, ENGLISH WRITER, COMMENTATOR, CRICKETER AND CAPTAIN

If I had to put it into
one word? Integrity.

DONALD BRADMAN, AUSTRALIAN CRICKETER,
ON HOW HE WANTED TO BE REMEMBERED

———◆●◆———

I regret that my mouth
overtakes my brain.

DERMOT REEVE, ENGLISH CRICKETER AND SOMERSET COACH

———◆●◆———

I passed him [Cowdrey] and Bailey
as they went in on Friday morning.
I murmured 'Good luck'. Cowdrey
said 'Thank you, sir'; Bailey said
nothing. In five balls Bailey was
out and in five hours Cowdrey
had made 152. The god of
cricket likes good manners.

GEORGE LYTTELTON, ENGLISH TEACHER AND ESSAYIST

COACHES AND CAPTAINS

Have nothing to do with coaches. In fact, if you should see one coming, go and hide behind the pavilion until he goes away.

BILL O'REILLY, AUSTRALIAN CRICKETER

Professional coaching is a
man trying to get your legs
close together when other men
had spent a lifetime trying
to get them wider apart.

RACHAEL HEYHOE-FLINT, ENGLISH CRICKET JOURNALIST
AND CAPTAIN OF THE ENGLISH LADIES XI

If I had my way, I would take him
to Traitor's Gate and personally
hang, draw and quarter him.

IAN BOTHAM, ENGLISH COMMENTATOR, TELEVISION
PERSONALITY AND CRICKETER, ON RAY ILLINGWORTH

I was never coached. I was
never told how to hold a bat.

DONALD BRADMAN

Pray God no professional
may ever captain England.

LORD HAWKE, ENGLISH CRICKETER

———•••———

Amateurs have always made,
and always will make, the best
captains, and this is only natural.

ALLAN GIBSON STEEL, ENGLISH CRICKETER

———•••———

Captaincy is 90 per cent luck
and 10 per cent skill. But don't
try it without that 10 per cent.

RICHIE BENAUD, AUSTRALIAN COMMENTATOR AND CRICKETER

Playing against a team with
Ian Chappell as captain turns a
cricket match into gang warfare.

MIKE BREARLEY, ENGLISH CRICKET
JOURNALIST AND ENGLAND CAPTAIN

———— •••• ————

You'll have the most miserable
time of your life.

BRIAN CLOSE, ENGLISH CRICKETER, TO
IAN BOTHAM ON CAPTAINCY

———— •••• ————

Being the manager of a
touring team is rather like
being in charge of a cemetery
– lots of people underneath
you, but no one listening.

WES HALL, BARBADIAN CRICKETER AND POLITICIAN

COMMENTATOR CLASSICS

It's been a very slow and dull day, but it hasn't been boring. It's been a good, entertaining day's cricket.

TONY BENNEWORTH, AUSTRALIAN CRICKET COMMENTATOR

Welcome to Worcester where we have just seen Barry Richards hit one of Basil D'Oliveira's balls clean out of the ground.

BRIAN JOHNSTON, ENGLISH CRICKET COMMENTATOR

Neil Harvey's at slip, with his legs wide apart, waiting for a tickle.

BRIAN JOHNSTON

Turner looks a bit shaky and unsteady, but I think he's going to bat on – one ball left.

BRIAN JOHNSTON

Welcome to Leicester, where
the captain Ray Illingworth
has just relieved himself
at the Pavilion End.

BRIAN JOHNSTON

— • • —

This bowler's like my dog:
three short legs and balls
that swing each way.

BRIAN JOHNSTON

Fred Titmus has
two short legs, one
of them square.

BRIAN JOHNSTON

Matthew Fleming used to
be in the Green Jackets,
but the way he's batting
suggests he'd be better suited
in the Light Brigade.

CHARLES COLVILLE, ENGLISH SPORTS COMMENTATOR

The Queen's Park Oval,
exactly as the name suggests,
absolutely round.

TONY CROZIER, WEST INDIAN CRICKET COMMENTATOR

England have nothing to lose
here, apart from this Test match.

DAVID LLOYD, ENGLISH COMMENTATOR AND CRICKETER

A very small crowd here today.
I can count the people on one
hand. Can't be more than 30.

MICHAEL ABRAHAMSON, SOUTH AFRICAN
CRICKET COMMENTATOR

Yorkshire all out 232, Hutton
ill – I'm sorry, Hutton 111.

JOHN SNAGGE, ENGLISH NEWSREADER AND COMMENTATOR

I've never got to the
bottom of streaking.

JONATHAN AGNEW, ENGLISH CRICKET
COMMENTATOR AND CRICKETER

There was a slight
interruption there
for athletics.

RICHIE BENAUD ON AN INVADING STREAKER

His throw went absolutely
nowhere near where it was going.

RICHIE BENAUD

———•●•———

He's usually a good puller – but
he couldn't get it up that time.

RICHIE BENAUD

———•●•———

The slow motion replay doesn't
show how fast that delivery was.

RICHIE BENAUD

Laird has been brought in to stand in the corner of the circle.

RICHIE BENAUD

⚫━━◆⚫◆━━

It was an excellent performance in the field, marred only when Harris dropped Crapp in the outfield.

BBC COMMENTATOR ON A MISSED CHANCE FROM AUSTRALIAN CRICKETER LINDSAY CRAPP

⚫━━◆⚫◆━━

If you go in with two fast bowlers and one breaks down, you're left two short.

BOB MASSIE, AUSTRALIAN RADIO COMMENTATOR AND CRICKETER

Those who run cricket in
this country, especially
at the domestic level, are
for the most part a self-
serving, pusillanimous and
self-important bunch of
myopic dinosaurs unable to
take any but the shortest-
term view of anything.

HENRY BLOFELD, ENGLISH CRICKET COMMENTATOR

In the rear, the small diminutive
figure of Shoaib Mohammed,
who can't be much taller
or shorter than he is. It's a
catch he would have caught
99 times out of a 1,000.

HENRY BLOFELD

Here comes Cunis –
his bowling, like his
name, neither one
thing nor the other.

BBC COMMENTATOR ON BOB CUNIS

CRICKET AND SOCIETY

Cricket – it's more than a game. It's an institution.

THOMAS HUGHES, ENGLISH LAWYER AND AUTHOR

Cricket brings the most opposite characters and the most diverse lives together. Anything that puts very many different kinds of people on a common ground must promote sympathy and kindly feelings.

KUMAR RANJITSINHJI, INDIAN CRICKETER

⚫●⚫

It is more than a game this cricket, it somehow holds up a mirror to English society.

NEVILLE CARDUS, ENGLISH JOURNALIST

The very word 'cricket' has become a synonym for all that is true and honest. To say 'that is not cricket' implies something underhand, something not in keeping with the best ideals.

PELHAM WARNER, ENGLISH CRICKETER

As every soldier has the baton of a field marshal in his knapsack, so every player has the bat of Lillywhite in his portmanteau.

WISDEN CRICKETERS' ALMANACK

Cricket is peculiarly a
Christian game. No pagan
nation has ever played it.

MELBOURNE NEWSPAPER

———•••———

Oh, I am so glad that you have
begun to take an interest in
cricket. It is simply a social
necessity in England.

P. G. WODEHOUSE, ENGLISH AUTHOR

———•••———

Cricket, like the upper classes
and standards in general,
is in permanent decline.

ALAN ROSS, ENGLISH POET AND EDITOR

We are nostalgic for the game's past, as well as our own. Some day, I suppose some will look fondly back on boozy, can-rattling spectators, players' rude and self-congratulatory gestures, shirts proper to squash net cricket, helmets less appropriate to Lord's than to Squires Gate.

ROY FULLER, ENGLISH AUTHOR AND POET

Innovations invariably are suspect and in no quarter more so than the cricket world.

GILBERT JESSOP, ENGLISH CRICKETER

If you made him prime minister tomorrow, he'd pick this country up in ten minutes.

BILLY ALLEY, AUSTRALIAN UMPIRE AND CRICKETER, ON IAN BOTHAM

———•••———

If Botham is an English folk hero, then this must be an alarming time for the nation.

DAVID MILLER, ENGLISH SPORTS JOURNALIST

———•••———

Cricket's greatness lies in the ability of players to honour a foe. It's the way life should be lived.

PROFESSOR WILLIAM BARCLAY, SCOTTISH AUTHOR AND THEOLOGIAN

CRICKET BATS AT DAWN: FIGHTING WORDS

Stuff that stiff upper lip crap. Let's see how stiff it is when it's split.

JEFF THOMPSON

Fred Trueman is bowling. The batsman edges and the ball goes to first slip, and right between Raman Subba Row's legs. At the end of the over, Row ambles past Trueman and apologises.
Row: 'I should've kept my legs together, Fred.'
Trueman: 'Not you, son. Your mother should've!'

———◆◆◆———

So how's your wife, and my kids?

ROD MARSH, AUSTRALIAN CRICKETER, TO IAN BOTHAM DURING A MATCH FROM BEHIND THE STUMPS

I know why he's bought a house by the sea... so he'll be able to go for a walk on the water.

FRED TRUEMAN ON GEOFF BOYCOTT'S MOVE TO POOLE HARBOUR

As Daryll Cullinan was on his way to the wicket, Shane Warne told him he had been waiting 2 years for another chance to humiliate him. Cullinan: 'Looks like you spent it all eating.'

During a Test match in the West Indies, Merv Hughes didn't say a word to Viv Richards, but continued to stare at him after deliveries. Richards: 'This is my island, my culture. Don't you be staring at me. In my culture we just bowl.' Merv didn't reply, but after he dismissed him he announced to the batsman: 'In my culture we just say "fuck off".'

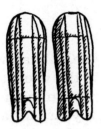

CRICKETERS ON CRICKETERS

Geoffrey is the only
fellow I've met who
fell in love with
himself at a young
age and has remained
faithful ever since.

DENNIS LILLEE ON GEOFF BOYCOTT

I remember the first time I walked into the Lancashire dressing room, when I was 16, all these guys – Atherton, Fairbrother, Akram – you just drop your shopping, you don't know where to put yourself. With Botham, I could barely pick my shopping up.

ANDREW FLINTOFF, ENGLISH CRICKETER, ON THE FIRST TIME HE MET IAN BOTHAM

A natural mistimer of the ball.

ANGUS FRASER ON MICHAEL ATHERTON

I don't know what these fellows
are doing, but whatever they are
doing, they sure are doing it well.

PETE SAMPRAS, AMERICAN TENNIS PLAYER, ON WATCHING
BRIAN LARA AND CURTLY AMBROSE AT LORD'S

———— •••• ————

I don't suppose I can call you a
lucky bleeder when you've got 347.

ANGUS FRASER, ENGLISH CRICKETER, TO BRIAN LARA

———— •••• ————

Off the field, he could be
your lifelong buddy, but
out in the middle, he had
all the loveable qualities of
a demented rhinoceros.

COLIN McCOOL, AUSTRALIAN CRICKETER, ON BILL O'REILLY

If it had been a cheese roll, it would never have got past him.

GRAHAM GOOCH, ENGLAND CRICKET CAPTAIN, ON MIKE GATTING BEING BOWLED OUT IN THE 1993 OLD TRAFFORD TEST

One of the few men capable
of looking more dishevelled
at the start of a six-hour
century than at the end of it.

MARTIN JOHNSON, ENGLISH CRICKET JOURNALIST,
ON MICHAEL ATHERTON AFTER HIS CENTURY AT
EDGBASTON AGAINST SOUTH AFRICA IN 1998

Eeyore without the *joie de vivre*.

MIKE SELVEY ON ANGUS FRASER

Hogg suggested we survey
the back of the Adelaide Oval,
and I don't think he had a
tennis match on his mind.

GRAHAM YALLOP, AUSTRALIAN CRICKETER, ON A DIFFERENCE
OF OPINION WITH HIS TEAMMATE RODNEY HOGG

If there were 22 Trevor Baileys
playing in a match, who
would ever go and watch it?

ARTHUR MORRIS, AUSTRALIAN CRICKETER

———— ●●● ————

Botham just couldn't
quite get his leg over.

JONATHAN AGNEW, ON IAN BOTHAM TRYING TO LIFT
HIS LEG OVER THE STUMPS WHEN OFF BALANCE

CRICKETERS V THE PRESS

If there is a game
that attracts the half-
baked theorists more
than cricket, I have
yet to hear of it.

FRED TRUEMAN

Cricket is full of theorists who can ruin your game in no time.

IAN BOTHAM

They smile and then they stab.

GEOFF BOYCOTT

Generally, the people out on the pitch are the ones who know how to play the game, not the ones who are writing about it.

MARCUS TRESCOTHICK, ENGLISH CRICKETER

Mark Waugh's a great friend
of mine and he's got to make
a few quid somehow, even
by joining you blokes.

SHANE WARNE, AUSTRALIAN CRICKETER,
SPEAKING TO THE PRESS

•••

If I had my time over again, I
would never have played cricket.
Why? Because of people like you.
The press do nothing but criticise.

GARRY SOBERS, WEST INDIAN CRICKETER

•••

I will never be accepted
by the snob press.

RAY ILLINGWORTH, ENGLISH CRICKET
COMMENTATOR AND CRICKETER

I have grown to trust and like several of the cricket writers. Equally, there are some I trust, but don't like, others I like, but don't trust and the occasional individual I neither like nor trust.

BOB WILLIS

———◆●●◆———

The media make mountains from molehills to satisfy producers and editors alike.

MARK NICHOLAS, ENGLISH COMMENTATOR AND CRICKETER

Newspapers are only good
enough for wrapping
up fish and chips.

MARTIN CROWE, NEW ZEALAND CRICKETER

———•••———

You buggers have been
lampooning me and
harpooning me.

TED DEXTER, ENGLISH CRICKETER, TO ASSEMBLED MEDIA

———•••———

They find a ghost in everything.

SHAKOOR RANA, PAKISTANI UMPIRE, ON THE ENGLISH TABLOIDS

You have to try to reply
to criticism with your
intellect, not your ego.

MIKE BREARLEY ON HANDLING THE MEDIA

———•●●———

England's tour of the
West Indies in 1986.
British Airways steward:
'Would you like me to take
anything home for you?'
Bob Willis, England captain:
'Yes, 34 journalists and
two camera crews.'

ENGLISH CRICKET

Cricket has been played pretty solidly in this country, and indeed throughout the Empire ever since the Norman Conquest, except perhaps during the Dark Ages, when bad light stopped play.

ANONYMOUS

English cricket, once a byword
for order and efficiency, with
sporadic exhibitions of genius,
is today – as Sir Denis Thatcher
might crisply put it – about
as much use as a one-legged
man at an arse-kicking party.

PROFILE OF THE ENGLAND CRICKET TEAM, *THE SUNDAY TIMES*

I can't bat, can't bowl and can't
field these days. I've every chance
of being picked for England.

RAY EAST, ENGLISH CRICKETER

If they want me to get
down to 12 stone, I would
have to cut off a leg.

IAN BLACKWELL, 17-STONE ENGLISH ALL-ROUNDER, ON THE
ENGLAND SELECTORS' ORDERS FOR HIM TO LOSE WEIGHT

———◦●◦———

You can't have 11 Darren
Goughs in your side – it would
drive you nuts. It would be
like having 11 Phil Tufnells.

DARREN GOUGH ON THE FUTURE OF ENGLAND'S BOWLING ATTACK

———◦●◦———

Many Continentals think
life is a game; the English
think cricket is a game.

GEORGE MIKES, HUNGARIAN-BORN BRITISH AUTHOR

Our cricket is too
gentle – all of it.

ALEC STEWART, ENGLISH CRICKETER AND ENGLAND CAPTAIN

— ●●● —

In an England cricket 11, the
flesh may be of the south, but
the bone is of the north and
the backbone is Yorkshire.

LEONARD HUTTON

— ●●● —

It has been said of the unseen
army of the dead, on their
everlasting march, that when
they are passing a rural cricket
ground, the Englishmen fall
out of the ranks for a moment
to lean over a gate and smile.

J. M. BARRIE

John Henry Newman was as
English as roast beef, even if he
lacked a passion for cricket.

CLIFFORD LONGLEY, ENGLISH JOURNALIST

———— •• • ————

Is there no way in which
Richards of Hampshire could be
co-opted into the English Test
side? Can no patriotic English
girl be persuaded to marry
him? He is quite personable...
Failing that, could not some
elderly gentleman adopt him?

THE TIMES

———— •• • ————

Bloody medieval most of them.

IAN BOTHAM ON THE ENGLISH CRICKET ADMINISTRATION

England will win if
Camilla Parker bowls.

AUSTRALIAN FANS' BANNER

During the ICC Trophy many of
the teams conversed on the field
in foreign tongues with the odd
cricket phrase coming through
in English. One such side was
Israel – a really happy band of
village standard players – from
whose chatter I suddenly picked
up the term 'in-swinger'. On
asking their Jewish captain as to
why he had no translation for this
type of delivery, he informed me
that this was because nobody had
bowled in the Old Testament.

GORDON HEWITT, JOURNALIST

Where the English language
is unspoken there can
be no real cricket.

NEVILLE CARDUS

———————•◉•———————

There have always been many
cricket cultures and those who
try and narrow it down to one,
who always claim to be the
defenders of some inner purity,
are the enemies of the game.

MIKE MARQUSEE, AMERICAN WRITER,
JOURNALIST AND POLITICAL ACTIVIST

———————•◉•———————

A few years ago England
would have struggled to
beat the Eskimos.

IAN BOTHAM

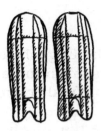

ENGLAND V AUSTRALIA

In Affectionate Remembrance
of English Cricket, which died
at The Oval on 29th August,
1882, Deeply lamented by a
large circle of sorrowing friends
and acquaintances. RIP.
NB – The body will be cremated
and the ashes taken to Australia.

SATIRICAL OBITUARY PUBLISHED IN *THE SPORTING TIMES*,
1882, FOLLOWING ENGLAND'S DEFEAT TO AUSTRALIA. THE
ENGLISH MEDIA THEN DUBBED THE NEXT ENGLISH TOUR
TO AUSTRALIA AS 'THE QUEST TO REGAIN THE ASHES' AND
THE TOURNAMENT AS IT IS KNOWN TODAY WAS BORN

Maybe it's the tally-ho attitude.
You know, there'll always be
an England, all that Empire
crap they dish out. But I
never could cop the Poms.

JEFF THOMPSON

Australian fans will have gone
to bed at three in the morning
knowing the sun will still come up
in the morning, but you don't like
losing to England at anything.

GEOFF LAWSON, AUSTRALIAN JOURNALIST AND CRICKETER

The aim of English Test cricket is, in fact, mainly to beat Australia.

JIM LAKER, ENGLISH CRICKETER

———•••———

If the Poms bat first, let's tell the taxi to wait.

AUSTRALIAN FANS' BANNER

———•••———

You know you're in Melbourne when you're walking through the park and you see someone kicking the footy with cricket pads on.

HUNG LE, AUSTRALIAN COMEDIAN

A fart competing with thunder.

GRAHAM GOOCH, ON AN ENGLAND V
AUSTRALIA MATCH IN 1991

Well, Andrew Strauss is
certainly an optimist – he's
come out wearing sunblock.

AUSTRALIAN COMMENTATOR, ON THE FIFTH TEST
OF THE 5-0 SERIES WHITEWASH IN 2006-07

FASTBALLS: QUICK QUIPS

I'd have looked even
faster in colour.

FRED TRUEMAN

David Gower:
'Do you want Gatting
a foot wider?'
Chris Cowdrey:
'No. He'd burst.'

DURING THE 1985 INDIA V ENGLAND TEST IN CALCUTTA

I've done the elephant.
I've done the poverty.
I might as well go home.

PHIL TUFNELL, DURING ENGLAND'S TOUR OF INDIA

———•••———

A dry fart!

PHIL EDMONDS, ENGLISH CRICKETER, ON BEING
ASKED WHAT HE LOOKED FORWARD TO MOST UPON
RETURNING FROM A LONG TOUR OF INDIA

———•••———

I just want to get into the middle
and get the right sort of runs.

ROBIN SMITH, SOUTH AFRICAN CRICKETER, ON
SUFFERING FROM DIARRHOEA ON TOUR IN INDIA

Ken Barrington: 'Let's cut out some of the quick singles.'
Fred Titmus: 'OK! We'll cut out yours, Ken.'

DURING A MID-WICKET CONFERENCE IN A TEST MATCH

———— •●• ————

In the 1991 Adelaide Test against Pakistan Merv Hughes was less than impressed when Javed Miandad called him a 'fat bus conductor' as the pair squared up to one another. A few balls later, Hughes got his man and as Javed walked past, could not resist shouting, 'Tickets, please!'

Merv Hughes.

STEVE WAUGH, AUSTRALIAN CRICKETER, ON BEING
ASKED WHAT HIS FAVOURITE ANIMAL WAS

———•◦•———

Dustin Hoffman and some Aussie
bowlers in the act of appealing.

DARRYL CULLINAN ON BEING ASKED WHO
HIS FAVOURITE ACTORS WERE

———•◦•———

It can't have been Gatt. Anything
he takes up to his room after
nine o'clock, he eats.

IAN BOTHAM COMMENTING ON MIKE GATTING
AND THE 'BARMAID AFFAIR'

GOOD DAYS AND BAD

If my grandfather
was alive, he
would have
slaughtered a cow.

MAKHAYA NTINI, SOUTH AFRICAN CRICKETER, AFTER TAKING
FIVE FOR 75 IN THE SECOND TEST AGAINST ENGLAND AT LORD'S

Yesterday at The Oval had to be the most thrilling moment of my life... perhaps after the birth of my children.

GLADSTONE SMALL, ENGLISH CRICKETER, ON THE ENGLAND ASHES WIN OF 2005

• • •

I can't really say I'm batting badly. I'm not batting long enough to be batting badly.

GREG CHAPPELL, AUSTRALIAN CRICKETER

• • •

You should play every game as if it's your last, but make sure you perform well enough to ensure that it's not.

JOHN EMBUREY, ENGLISH CRICKETER

It's a bit like the four-minute mile or climbing Mount Everest. Someone is going to do it eventually, but no one forgets the person who did it first.

RICHARD HADLEE, NEW ZEALAND CRICKETER, ON BEING FIRST TO SCORE 400 TEST WICKETS

●●●

In real cricket, the player who has developed imagination and skill makes the game, but in the one-day match it is the other way around. The match dictates to the player.

BRIAN CLOSE

The game you are frightened of losing is not worth winning.

BENNY GREEN, BRITISH JAZZ SAXOPHONIST AND WRITER

I'm very concerned for our middle order. We've already called on the immediate next people down, so who do you go to next? I've got a four-year-old son who might like a go.

KEN RUTHERFORD, NEW ZEALAND CRICKETER, AFTER A BIG DEFEAT BY AUSTRALIA IN 1993

The way to do it is enjoy your cricket and relax, to accept occasionally you'll have a bad day and try to get out of bed with a smile on your face.

GRAEME THORPE, ENGLISH CRICKETER

———◦●◦———

I always played to win.

HANSIE CRONJE, SOUTH AFRICAN CRICKETER

———◦●◦———

Any time the West Indies lose, I cry.

LANCE GIBBS, WEST INDIAN CRICKETER

I play best when I'm surrounded by people who appreciate me.

GEOFF BOYCOTT

Bowl better and bat better.

RICKY PONTING, AUSTRALIAN CRICKETER, ON HOW
AUSTRALIA CAN IMPROVE THEIR PERFORMANCE

———————•••———————

Only two problems with our
team. Brewer's droop and
financial cramp. Apart from that
we ain't bloody good enough.

CHARLIE PARKER, ENGLISH CRICKETER

———————•••———————

You are only as good as
your last game.

IAN BOTHAM

I think we are all slightly down in the dumps after another loss. We may be in the wrong sign… Venus may be in the wrong juxtaposition with somewhere else.

TED DEXTER EXPLAINING AWAY ENGLAND'S SEVENTH SUCCESSIVE TEST LOSS TO AUSTRALIA AT LORD'S, 1993

• ◆ •

Nobody's perfect. You know what happened to the last man who was – they crucified him.

GEOFF BOYCOTT

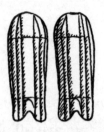

IS THAT WHAT THEY MEANT TO SAY?

I've seen batting all
over the world. And in
other countries, too.

KEITH MILLER, AUSTRALIAN CRICKETER

It's tough for a natural
hooker to give it up.

IAN CHAPPELL, AUSTRALIAN CRICKETER

———•••———

I condone anyone who
tampers with the ball.

ALLAN LAMB, SOUTH AFRICAN-BORN ENGLISH CRICKETER,
WHO MAY JUST HAVE MEANT 'CONDEMN'

———•••———

Anyone foolish enough
to predict the outcome of
this match is a fool.

FRED TRUEMAN

The bowler's Holding,
the batsman's Willey.

BRIAN JOHNSTON, ON PETER WILLEY AND
MICHAEL HOLDING FACING EACH OTHER

———•••———

Unless something happens
that we can't predict, I don't
think a lot will happen.

FRED TRUEMAN

———•••———

There were congratulations
and high-sixes all round.

RICHIE BENAUD

On the first day, Logie decided to chance his arm and it came off.

TREVOR BAILEY, ENGLISH CRICKETER

————●●●————

Strangely, in slow-motion replay, the ball seemed to hang in the air for even longer.

DAVID ACFIELD, ENGLISH CRICKETER

————●●●————

Against Surrey, tomorrow, Somerset will beat Middlesex.

LLOYD'S WEEKLY

Reporter: 'Do you feel that the selectors and yourself have been vindicated by the result?'
Gatting: 'I don't think the press are vindictive. They can write what they want.'

———•••———

We've won one on the trot.

ALEC STEWART

THE JOYS OF CRICKET

Watching cricket has given me
more happiness than any other
activity in which I have engaged.
Lord's on a warm day, with a
bottle, a mixed bag of sandwiches,
and a couple of spare tyres in
a despatch case, and I don't
care who is playing whom.

A. A. MILNE, ENGLISH AUTHOR

There is no talk, none so witty
and brilliant, that is so good
as cricket talk, when memory
sharpens memory, and the dead
live again – the regretted, the
forgotten – and the old happy
days of burned out Junes revive.

ANDREW LANG, SCOTTISH POET AND NOVELIST

Cricket is indescribable. How
do you describe an orgasm?

GREG MATTHEWS, AUSTRALIAN CRICKETER

To go to a cricket match for
nothing but cricket is as
though a man were to go into
an inn for nothing but drink.

NEVILLE CARDUS

The love of cricket nowadays seems to be confined to those who watch it or read about it.

ARTHUR MAILEY, AUSTRALIAN CRICKETER

But after all, it's not the winning that matters, is it? Or is it? It's — to coin a word — the amenities that count: the smell of the dandelions, the puff of the pipe, the click of the bat, the rain on the neck, the chill down the spine, the slow, exquisite coming on of sunset and dinner and rheumatism.

ALASTAIR COOKE, ENGLISH-BORN AMERICAN
JOURNALIST AND BROADCASTER

In my opinion cricket is too great a game to think about statistically.

E. H. HENDREN, ENGLISH CRICKETER

If I knew I was going to die today, I'd still want to hear the cricket scores.

J. H. HARDY

LADIES AND CRICKET

We have nothing
against man
cricketers. Some of
them are quite nice
people, even though
they don't win as
often as we do.

RACHAEL HEYHOE-FLINT

When we were living in Sydney a friend told me that one night, while she and her husband were making love, she suddenly noticed something sticking in his ear. When she asked him what it was he replied, 'Be quiet! I'm listening to the cricket.'

VICKY RANTZEN, JOURNALIST

How can the ladies hurt their delicate fingers, and even bring them to blisters, with holding a nasty filthy bat? How can their sweet delicate fingers bear the jarrings attending the catching of a dirty ball?

THE 3RD DUKE OF DORSET IN RESPONSE TO THE PROPOSITION THAT WOMEN BE ALLOWED TO PLAY CRICKET

A loving wife is better than
making 50 in cricket, or even
99; beyond that I will not go.

J. M. BARRIE

———•••———

Women are for batsmen,
beer is for bowlers. God
help the all-rounders.

FRED TRUEMAN

———•••———

Ladies playing cricket – absurd.
Just like a man trying to knit.

LEONARD HUTTON

The MCC should change
their name to the MCP.

DIANA EDULJI, INDIAN WOMEN'S CAPTAIN, CALLING THE
MARYLEBONE CRICKET CLUB MALE CHAUVINIST PIGS
AFTER BEING REFUSED ENTRY TO THE LORD'S PAVILION

———•●•———

Popular opinion would be wrong if
it ever thought that the M in MCC
could stand for misogyny. Quite
the reverse is the case. But it may
well be that in this changing world
there would be one small part
of London which affords refuge
for the hunted male animal.

JACK BAILEY, ENGLISH CRICKETER AND MCC SECRETARY

The days of women's cricket
being seen as a knicker
parade must be over.

NORMA IZARD, ENGLAND MANAGER AND ONE OF THE
FIRST FEMALE MEMBERS OF MCC, ON THE ENGLAND
WOMEN'S CRICKET TEAM WINNING THE WORLD CUP

———•••———

The crack of the bat against
the ball amid the humming
and buzzing… is still to me
a note of pure joy that raises
haunting memories of friends
and happy days. The one
game in the world for me.

LUCY BALDWIN, MEMBER OF THE WHITE
HEATHER CRICKET CLUB

My friend Imran Khan, who is a famous cricketer and a very popular man with the ladies, has bodyguards outside his room, warding women off. I have guys warding them in.

ZIA MAHMOOD, PAKISTANI BRIDGE PLAYER

Women find it more than difficult not to cross and uncross their legs under his gaze.

LORD TIM HUDSON, ENGLISH ECCENTRIC, ON THE SEX APPEAL OF IAN BOTHAM

———————•●●•———————

The authorities should consider that a cricketer is more likely to have a proper night's sleep with his wife in bed beside him, rather than a temporary stand-in and all the parallel gymnastics that would follow.

LINDSAY LAMB, WIFE OF ALLAN LAMB

I only got into the game
as a roving hockey player
looking for something to do
in the summer, and having
an older brother helps.

LUCY PEARSON, ENGLISH CRICKETER

• ● •

Pitches are like wives – you
can never tell how they're
going to turn out.

LEONARD HUTTON

• ● •

I always thought I'd play cricket
for Australia, I just never thought
it would be in the women's team.

CATHRYN FITZPATRICK, AUSTRALIAN CRICKETER

LITERARY CRICKET

Capital gain –
smart sport – fine
exercise – very.

CHARLES DICKENS, ENGLISH WRITER, ON CRICKET

Baseball and cricket are
beautiful and highly stylised
medieval war substitutes,
chess made flesh, a mixture
of proud chivalry and base
– in both senses – greed.

JOHN FOWLES, ENGLISH NOVELIST AND ESSAYIST

I don't think I can be expected
to take seriously a game which
takes less than three days
to reach its conclusion.

TOM STOPPARD, CZECHOSLOVAKIAN-BORN ENGLISH
PLAYWRIGHT, REJECTING BASEBALL IN FAVOUR OF CRICKET

It's not in support of cricket but
as an earnest protest against golf.

MAX BEERBOHM, ENGLISH CRITIC, ESSAYIST AND
CARICATURIST, WHEN ASKED TO CONTRIBUTE
TO W. G. GRACE'S TESTIMONIAL

Strolling about the theatre one evening, he said on seeing me, 'Oh! Hicks, do you play cricket?' I said, 'Yes I do, Mr Barrie.' 'Well, will you come down to Sandwich and play against the fire brigade men for me?' he enquired. I said I should be delighted, but it would be impossible as I should be unable to get back to London in time to act that night. 'Oh, don't bother about that,' said Barrie, 'we can put on the understudy.'

SEYMOUR HICKS, ENGLISH ACTOR, RECALLING THE TIME HE PLAYED THE PART OF ANDREW MCPHAIL, THE MEDICAL STUDENT, IN J. M. BARRIE'S PLAY *WALKER LONDON* AT TOOLE'S THEATRE

Sir Donald Bradman
Would have been a very glad man
If his Test average had
been .06 more
Than 99.94.

T. N. E. SMITH

●●●

As in life so in death lies
a bat of renown,
Slain by a lorry (three ton);
His innings is over, his
bat is laid down;
To the end a poor judge of a run.

INSCRIPTION ON AN ENGLISH GRAVESTONE

Cricket is full of glorious chances, and the Goddess who presides over it loves to bring down the most skilful player.

THOMAS HUGHES

———•●●•———

I see them in foul dug-
outs, gnawed by rats,
And lying in the ruined
temples, lashed by rain,
Dreaming of things they
did with balls and bats.

SIEGFRIED SASSOON, ENGLISH SOLDIER AND POET, WHO
LIVED AS A COUNTRY GENTLEMAN, HUNTING AND PLAYING
CRICKET, BEFORE BEING SENT TO FIGHT IN WORLD WAR ONE

You know Lord's? Well,
once I played there
And a ball I hit to leg
Struck the umpire's
head, stayed there
As a nest retains an egg.

HARRY GRAHAM, ENGLISH POET

Looking backward we could
almost see, suspended with
the most delicate equipoise
above the flat little island, the
ghostly shapes of those twin
orbs of the Empire, the cricket
ball and the black ball.

PATRICK LEIGH FERMOR, ENGLISH
AUTHOR, SCHOLAR AND SOLDIER

We didn't have any metaphors
in my day. We didn't
beat about the bush.

FRED TRUEMAN

●◆●

Thy fame has spread
wherever bat and ball
Ring with their joyous
clatter o'er the field.
On this thy birthday
may no shadow fall
And may it still a further
hundrevd yield;
Thou art the centre
of a million eyes
Who love one summer
game and sunny skies.

J. P. KINGSTON, 'TO W. G. GRACE', TO
COMMEMORATE HIS JUBILEE

There's a breathless hush
in the Close tonight –
Ten to make and a match to win –
A bumping pitch and
a blinding light,
An hour to play and
the last man in.
And it's not for the sake
of a ribboned coat,
Or the selfish hope of
a season's fame,
But his Captain's hand on
his shoulder smote –
'Play up! play up! and
play the game!'

HENRY NEWBOLT, ENGLISH AUTHOR AND POET

We have played Eton and were
most confoundedly beat, however
it was some comfort to me that
I got 11 notches in the first
innings and seven the second...

LORD BYRON, ANGLO-SCOTTISH POET, IN A LETTER
REFERRING TO THE INITIAL MATCH IN A SERIES IN 1805.
BYRON'S ACTUAL SCORES WERE SOMEWHAT DIFFERENT

—— •◦• ——

I tend to believe that cricket
is the greatest thing that God
ever created on earth... certainly
greater than sex, although
sex isn't too bad either.

HAROLD PINTER, ENGLISH PLAYWRIGHT AND THEATRE DIRECTOR

—— •◦• ——

Alas, I don't even know enough
about cricket to attack it.
Anyway, I wouldn't attack it as I
much prefer it to muddied oafs.

GRAHAM GREENE, ENGLISH WRITER

Football offers the world clichés;
rugby produces facial deformity;
hockey provides an acceptable
outlet for psychotic violence;
cricket alone breeds myths.

ANONYMOUS

That Bill's a foolish fellow;
He has given me a black eye.
He does not know how to handle a bat
Any more than a dog, or a cat;
He has knock'd down the wicket,
And broken his stumps
And runs without shoes
to save his pumps.

WILLIAM BLAKE, ENGLISH POET

While batting once, the
Prince of Wales – whose
name was Frederick Louis,
Was hit upon the head, and so
his legs went soft and gooey.
He later died because he got
that bouncer to the brain,
So in this case you might say
the result was 'play stopped reign'.

RICHARD STILGOE, ENGLISH LYRICIST AND MUSICIAN

MISUNDERSTANDING CRICKET

Sometimes, people
think it's like polo,
played on horseback,
and I remember
one guy thought
it was a game
involving insects.

CLAYTON LAMBERT, WEST INDIAN CRICKETER,
EXPLAINING CRICKET TO AMERICANS

Basically it's just a
whole bunch of blokes
standing around
scratching themselves.

KATHY LETTE, AUSTRALIAN AUTHOR

It's a silly game that
nobody wins.

THOMAS FULLER, ENGLISH CLERGYMAN AND HISTORIAN

———— •●• ————

Generally regarded as an
incomprehensibly dull
and pointless game.

DOUGLAS ADAMS, ENGLISH RADIO DRAMATIST AND AUTHOR

———— •●• ————

I would rather watch a man at
his toilet than on a cricket field.

ROBERT MORLEY, ENGLISH ACTOR

Baseball has the great advantage over cricket of being ended sooner.

GEORGE BERNARD SHAW, IRISH LITERARY CRITIC, PLAYWRIGHT AND ESSAYIST

———◆◆◆———

Cricket? It's rubbish. I don't like it. It's not a very emotive game.

JUNINHO, BRAZILIAN FOOTBALLER

———◆◆◆———

Of course it's frightfully dull! That's the whole point!... To go to cricket to be thrilled is as stupid as to go to a Chekhov play in search of melodrama.

ROBERT MORLEY, *THE FINAL TEST*

A cricketer – a
creature very nearly
as stupid as a dog.

BERNARD LEVIN, ENGLISH JOURNALIST,
AUTHOR AND BROADCASTER

THE NATURE OF
THE GAME

Personally,
I have always
looked on cricket as
organised loafing.

WILLIAM TEMPLE, NINTH ARCHBISHOP OF CANTERBURY

Distrusting the arts, the English found a substitute in cricket – a timeless blend of formal dancing, rhetoric and comic opera.

KENNETH GREGORY

———•●•———

There is no more amateurish professional game in the world than cricket.

JOHN EMBUREY

———•●•———

Cricket is the easiest sport in the world to take over. Nobody bothered to pay the players what they were worth.

KERRY PACKER, AUSTRALIAN PUBLISHING, MEDIA AND GAMING TYCOON, COMMENTING ON THE FOUNDATION OF WORLD SERIES CRICKET

Cricket is certainly a very good and wholesome exercise, yet it may be abused if either great or little people make it their business.

THE GENTLEMAN'S MAGAZINE

Cricket is the only game I can enjoy without taking sides.

A. A. MILNE

Cricket's a game, not a competition.

GEORGE HIRST, ENGLISH CRICKETER

I'm not interested in sport. I'm interested in cricket. I'm always surprised to find cricket books in the library in the sports section, next to football.

JOHN MINNION, ENGLISH ILLUSTRATOR AND CAPTAIN OF THE *NEW STATESMAN* CRICKET SIDE

───•••───

We don't play this game for fun.

WILFRED RHODES, ENGLISH CRICKETER

───•••───

A Test match is like a painting. A one-day match is like a Rolf Harris painting.

IAN CHAPPELL

One-day cricket is like fast
food. No one wants to cook.

VIV RICHARDS, WEST INDIAN CRICKETER

One-day cricket is an exhibition.
Test cricket is an examination.

HENRY BLOFELD

Cricket is battle and service
and sport and art.

DOUGLAS JARDINE, ENGLISH CRICKETER

I've heard it said that this game at Test level is 50 per cent in the mind, 50 per cent in the mind, 50 per cent in the heart, and bugger technique, and that's not far off the mark.

RAY ILLINGWORTH

OFF THE PITCH

I have been to many
functions where some
great cricketers of the
past have been present.
To see some of them
sink their drink is to
witness performances
as awe-inspiring as ever
any of them displayed
on the cricket field.

IAN BOTHAM

If I'd done a quarter of the things of which I'm accused, I'd be pickled in alcohol. I'd be a registered drug addict and would have sired half the children in the world's cricket-playing countries.

IAN BOTHAM

• • •

When you have to spend the tour in your hotel room so you're not stitched up, there's something wrong.

IAN BOTHAM ON ENGLAND'S TOUR OF THE WEST INDIES

I'd rather face Dennis Lillee with a stick of rhubarb than go through all that again.

IAN BOTHAM, CLEARED OF ASSAULT CHARGES AT GRIMSBY CROWN COURT

Please don't make me
out to be a cad.

MARK NICHOLAS, SPEAKING TO THE PRESS AFTER
REVELATIONS ABOUT HIS PRIVATE LIFE

———•●•———

If it is embarrassing then it
is wrong, but if it is private,
and hopefully delightful, then
what could be better – even in
the middle of a Test Match?

TED DEXTER ON PLAYERS' NOCTURNAL ACTIVITIES IN
THE WAKE OF THE GATTING 'BARMAID AFFAIR'

THE PLAYERS

It is strange, but
I think true, that all the
time, day and night,
somewhere in the world
somebody is talking
about Bradman.

JACK INGHAM, AUSTRALIAN THOROUGHBRED HORSE-
BREEDER AND RACING ENTHUSIAST, ON DONALD BRADMAN

Surely Mr Adlard achieves a masterpiece of meiosis in saying that Gilbert Jessop 'should be included among the mighty hitters'? It is like saying that St. Peter's must find a place among the big churches of the world.

LAURENCE MEYNELL, ENGLISH AUTHOR

<hr>

The first rock and roll cricketer.

LEONARD HUTTON ON IAN BOTHAM

Difficult to be more
laid-back without being
actually comatose.

FRANCES EDMONDS, ENGLISH AUTHOR AND
BROADCASTER, ON DAVID GOWER

———•●•———

It's like watching a swan.
What you see on the surface
bears no relation to the activity
going on underneath.

DAVID GOWER ON BEING ACCUSED OF BEING TOO LAID-BACK

———•●•———

[He's got a] reputation for
being awkward and arrogant,
probably because he is
awkward and arrogant.

FRANCES EDMONDS, ON HER HUSBAND PHIL

Charles Wright was the Captain of Notts, and had also got a century in the University match. He was a most delightful person, but by no means the complete *Encyclopaedia Britannica.*

THE CRICKETER

Easy to watch, difficult to bowl to, and impossible to write about. When you bowled to him there weren't enough fielders; when you wrote about him there weren't enough words.

R. C. ROBERTSON-GLASGOW, ENGLISH CRICKETER AND CRICKET WRITER, ON FRANK WOOLLEY, *CRICKET PRINTS*

If someone wore a chocolate
bar on his head, Goughie
would follow suit.

STEVE OLDHAM, ENGLISH CRICKETER, ON DARREN GOUGH

The petty things of cricketing life
seem to be below Worrell. The
will to win at all costs is somehow
distasteful to him. The game,
not the result, means more.

RON ROBERTS, AUSTRALIAN RUGBY LEAGUE
PLAYER, ON FRANK WORRELL

Others scored faster; hit the
ball harder; more obviously
murdered bowling. No one
else, though, ever batted with
such consummate skill.

JOHN ARLOTT, ENGLISH SPORTS COMMENTATOR, ON JACK HOBBS

Denis Compton was the only
player to call his partner for
a run and wish him good
luck at the same time.

JOHN WARR, ENGLISH CRICKETER

———— •●• ————

When we were children we asked
my Uncle Charles what it was like
to play cricket with W. G. Grace.
'The dirtiest neck I ever kept
wicket behind,' was his crisp reply.

LORD CHANDOS

His personality was such that
it is remembered by those who
played with him to the exclusion
of his actual performance.

JOHN ARLOTT ON W. G. GRACE

— • • • —

Had Grace been born in ancient
Greece, *The Iliad* would have
been a different book.

THE BISHOP OF HEREFORD, QUOTED BY CLIFFORD BAX
IN *W. G. GRACE,* (*CRICKETING LIVES* SERIES)

POLITICIANS ON CRICKET

Cricket can be a
bridge and a glue...
Cricket for peace
is my mission.

MUHAMMAD ZIA-UL-HAQ, PRESIDENT OF PAKISTAN

158

You do well to love cricket, because it is more free from anything sordid, anything dishonourable than any game in the world. To play it keenly, generously, self-sacrificingly is a moral lesson in itself, and the classroom is God's air and sunshine. Foster it, my brothers, so that it may attract all who find the time to play it, protect it from anything that will sully it, so that it may grow in favour with all men.

LORD HARRIS, TRINDAD-BORN ENGLISH
POLITICIAN AND ENGLAND CAPTAIN

———•●•———

Australians will always fight for these 22 yards. Lord's and its traditions belong to Australia just as much as to England.

JOHN CURTIN, AUSTRALIAN PRIME
MINISTER, IN A SPEECH TO LORD'S

Mrs Thatcher is in the
position of a Martian trying
to understand cricket.

NEIL KINNOCK, WELSH POLITICIAN, REFERRING TO THE
THEN PRIME MINISTER'S ATTITUDE TOWARDS FOOTBALL
IDENTITY CARDS AND THE TAYLOR ENQUIRY

———•••———

Explaining the rules of
cricket is an excellent test
for high-powered brains.

JOHN MAJOR, BRITISH PRIME MINISTER

———•••———

Any cricketer would want
to bowl to Bradman even if
he were to hit them for six.
It's the same with Robin.

BRIAN WALDEN, ENGLISH JOURNALIST AND MP, ON ROBIN DAY
AND THE POLITICIANS QUEUING TO BE LASHED BY HIS TONGUE

Politics governs everything we do – the games we play, the way we play them, who we play.

JOHN ARLOTT

———•●•———

Cricket had plunged me into politics long before I was aware of it. When I did turn to politics I did not have too much to learn.

C. L. R. JAMES, TRINIDAD-BORN CRICKET JOURNALIST AND AUTHOR

Say that cricket has nothing to do with politics and you say that cricket has nothing to do with life.

JOHN ARLOTT

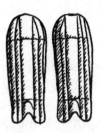

THE PRESENTATION
OF THE PLAYERS

It requires one
to assume such
indecent postures.

OSCAR WILDE, IRISH PLAYWRIGHT, NOVELIST AND POET

Some medical men... reprobate that of cricket as too violent — alleging, that the positions into which players must necessarily throw themselves cannot fail to be productive of injury to the body. Dislocations of the hip-joint are not uncommon, from the awkward posture occasioned by employing both arms at the same time in striking a distant object!

THE EUROPEAN MAGAZINE AND LONDON REVIEW ON AN EXCURSION TO BRIGHTON BY A CONTRIBUTOR TO THE MAGAZINE, JOHN EVANS, IN JULY 1818

• • •

If you can't always play like a cricketer, you can at least look like one.

DONALD BRADMAN

If you like a white sun hat,
always carry one with you.
C. B. Fry played some of his
greatest innings in a sun hat.

'CROSS-ARROW', *THE CRICKETER*

———•●•———

Maybe I should smile a bit more...
raise the profile and have a nice
spin-off contract for wearing
something or other. But that's
not me. I look like I do on the field
because what I do is knackering.

ANGUS FRASER

I doubt if many of my contemporaries, especially the older ones, did many exercises. I have often tried to picture [Godfrey] Evans and [Denis] Compton doing press-ups in the outfield before the day's play, but so far have failed miserably.

PETER MAY, ENGLISH CRICKETER

Cricket needs umpires who
grace the general scene with
sartorial sharpness, instead
of resembling a pair of Balkan
refugees clad by Oxfam.

JOHN SHEPPARD, WEST INDIAN CRICKETER

The gum-chewing habit
is very catching, and you
will sometimes see a whole
fielding team resembling a
herd of cows at pasture.

R. C. ROBERTSON-GLASGOW, ENGLISH CRICKETER

Chris Lewis baldly went where no other cricketer has gone before – and the prat without a hat spent two days in bed with sunstroke.

ANONYMOUS

THE PRESS STEP UP TO THE CREASE

Cricket must be
the only business
where you can make
more money on one
day than three.

PAT GIBSON, IRISH-BORN LEADING BRITISH QUIZ PLAYER

Bill Hudson lost 100 schooners of beer when he bet that Kevin Douglas Walters could not make 100 first time out against the Poms. Only when you have seen him bat and tested his self-possession do you realise how rash that wager really was.

IAN WOOLDRIDGE, ENGLISH SPORTS JOURNALIST

◆●◆

It was like seeing the future and realising that it worked.

STEVE BRENKLEY, ENGLISH JOURNALIST, ON BEN HOLLIOAKE, AUSTRALIAN-BORN ENGLISH CRICKETER

[Gower wore] an expression of permanent pained bewilderment, like a man who's just stepped into a lift-shaft.

MICHAEL HENDERSON, ENGLISH JOURNALIST, ON DAVID GOWER DURING A DERBY V LEICESTER GAME

[Courtney Walsh], who has effectively lost West Indies both their matches, was presented with a carpet for not running out Salim Jaffer off the final ball. He was last seen trying to fly home on it.

MARTIN JOHNSON

It was not unlike watching
Lazarus rise from the dead
and get mown down by a
runaway truck on his way to
meet his mates in the bar.

IAN WOOLDRIDGE ON NEW ZEALAND'S PERFORMANCE
AGAINST PAKISTAN IN THE 1992 WORLD CUP

●●●

It was perhaps inevitable
that your God-given talent
should be envied by those
who sweat in shell-suits to
achieve less dazzling results.
But who would have believed
that spite and stupidity could
have so hijacked the glorious
game? Corinth, it seems, has
given way to Chelmsford and
we are all the poorer for it.

FRANCES EDMONDS ON DAVID GOWER

At least we are safe from an intoxicated rendition of 'There's only one Graeme Hick'. There are, quite clearly, two of them. The first one turns out for teams like Worcestershire and New Zealand's Northern Districts and plays like a god. The second one pulls on an England cap and plays like the anagram of a god.

MARTIN JOHNSON

Here was English cricket's Messiah, preceded by Ian Botham's shaggy John the Baptist. Perhaps we should all have noticed that Hick became eligible to play for England on April Fool's day.

JOHN DUGDALE, ENGLISH JOURNALIST, ON GRAEME HICK

Alan Green, the occasional
off-spinner, might just turn a
spin-drier but not much else.

MIHIR BOSE, INDIAN JOURNALIST AND AUTHOR

• • •

Cricket on pitches like this
bears the same relationship
to the true first-class cricket
that target shooting bears
to Russian roulette.

MALCOLM WINTER, ON NORTHANTS V
WEST INDIES AT NORTHAMPTON

• • •

[Ilott] is out of this game with
a groin strain and thus joins
Darren Gough, Chris Lewis and
Andrew Caddick on the list of
those more in line for a trip to
Lourdes rather than Lord's.

MARTIN JOHNSON

Barring injuries or sexual indiscretions between now and next Thursday, the three other newcomers [Barnett, Russell and Lawrence] seem certain to get the benefit of the Peter May Emporium's giant 1988 England Cap Sale.

MATTHEW ENGEL, ENGLISH JOURNALIST

Watching Clinton steal a match in which Hick and Botham are playing is like going to a Pavarotti concert and seeing him upstaged by Des O'Connor.

MIKE SELVEY

[Ted Dexter], the most charismatic cricketer of his generation, who used to roar thro' the Lord's gates on a 1,000 cc motorbike, will phut-phut his way back out of them on a metaphorical moped, his public persona having altered – in the space of four and a half years – from a latter-day Lawrence of Arabia into something closer to Mr Magoo.

MARTIN JOHNSON

By close of play on Tuesday, having been set a target to win of just 194, England were 40 for eight off 14.5 overs. It was a collapse even more humiliating than that of John Major over voting rights in Brussels. Next morning, England's remaining wickets were taken quicker than a stray fiver in the Portobello Road. There were by now enough ducks on the field to feed an average family for a fortnight...

PROFILE OF THE ENGLAND CRICKET TEAM, *THE SUNDAY TIMES*

RETIREMENT

Endless cricket, like
endless anything
else, simply grinds
you down.

TED DEXTER

So I joined a Barclays Bank
graduate training scheme in
1991. People were amazed I
could contemplate such a swap.
I suppose it was like John Major
running away from his circus
background to be an accountant.

JOHN CARR, ENGLISH CRICKETER, ON HIS LEAVING
MIDDLESEX, AS REPORTED BY ROB STEEN

Golf is a game to be played
between cricket and death.

COLIN INGLEBY-MCKENZIE, ENGLISH CRICKETER

A bout of jaundice took the edge off my stamina once and for all and I realised then that human bodies are not like vintage motor cars. No amount of rebuilding and polishing has the same effect.

TED DEXTER

Ask me that again when you're all in Dhaka and I'm in Rome, watching Chelsea playing Lazio!

ALEC STEWART, ON BEING ASKED IF HE WOULD REGRET RETIRING

I've had about ten operations.
I'm a bit like a battered old
Escort. You might find one
panel left that's an original.

IAN BOTHAM

—•●•—

I won't miss bowling 20
overs uphill into the wind.

IAN BOTHAM

—•●•—

For many sportsmen, coming face-
to-face with irrefutable evidence
of their mortality is the moment
they dread above all others.

IAN BOTHAM

SCHOOLBOY CRICKET

Years lost in early
life are irrecoverable,
especially in cricket.

LES AMES, ENGLISH CRICKETER

When Merv leaves school, he is going to have to be very good at football and cricket.

AUSTRALIAN CRICKETER MERV HUGHES'
FIFTH-FORM GEOGRAPHY REPORT

———●●●———

Mike said that he'd read Wilbur Smith when he was eight. That's why he went to Cambridge and I didn't.

GRAEME HICK, ZIMBABWEAN CRICKETER,
ON HIS CAPTAIN MICHAEL ATHERTON

———●●●———

He's Biggles, the VC, El Alamein, the tank commander, he's everything. I mean, how could a schoolboy not want to be like Ian Botham?

LORD TIM HUDSON

Sometimes an unlucky
boy will drive his cricket
ball full in my face.

DR SAMUEL JOHNSON, ENGLISH POET, ESSAYIST,
BIOGRAPHER, LEXICOGRAPHER AND LITERARY CRITIC

———•●•———

I well remember… at my Big
School, after I missed a catch
at long-leg, saying to myself,
'O Lord take away my life, for
I am not worthy to live!'

JOHN COWPER POWYS, ENGLISH-WELSH
WRITER, LECTURER, AND PHILOSOPHER

A boy running hell for leather at
Winchester cannoned head down
into E. R. Wilson on his way to
school, looked up and in horror
gasped, 'Good God', to which
E. R. Wilson gently replied,
'But strictly incognito.'

GEORGE LYTTELTON, ENGLISH POLITICIAN AND AUTHOR

———●●●———

What's the point in
O Levels? They don't help
you play cricket!

IAN BOTHAM

Brian Johnston's cheeky wit did
not start and end with cricket.
While attending Oxford, he
was at a lecture on Henry V.
Professor: 'Now let us turn to
Henry's wife – Henrietta.'
Johnston, from the back of the
auditorium: 'Did he really, sir?'

THE WEATHER AND THE GROUNDS

The elements are cricket's presiding geniuses.

NEVILLE CARDUS

It is extremely cold here.
The England fielders are
keeping their hands in
pockets between balls.

CHRISTOPHER MARTIN-JENKINS, ENGLISH CRICKET
COMMENTATOR AND JOURNALIST

•••

I enjoyed it, but if I go back
again I'll wear a tin hat.

LAURIE LEE, ENGLISH POET AND NOVELIST, AFTER BEING
KNOCKED UNCONSCIOUS BY A FLYING BEER BOTTLE DURING
A GAME BETWEEN AUSTRALIA AND NEW ZEALAND

•••

Four separate stoppages
for rain and bad light left
the day as shapeless as a
Demis Roussos costume.

GLENN MOORE, ENGLISH JOURNALIST, ON KENT
V MIDDLESEX AT CANTERBURY IN 1994

What is both surprising and delightful is that spectators are allowed and even expected to join in the vocal part of the game... There is no reason why the field should not try to put the batsman off his stroke at the critical moment by neatly timed disparagements of his wife's fidelity and his mother's respectability.

GEORGE BERNARD SHAW

———•••———

Oh God! If there be cricket in heaven, let there also be rain.

ALEC DOUGLAS-HOME, BRITISH PRIME MINISTER

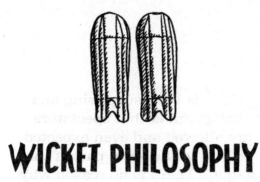

WICKET PHILOSOPHY

Ninety per cent of
cricket is played
in the mind.

RICHARD HADLEE

All is vanity, but cricket.

REVD JOHN MITFORD, EDITOR OF *THE GENTLEMAN'S MAGAZINE*

———•••———

The English are not very spiritual people, so they invented cricket to give them some idea of eternity.

GEORGE BERNARD SHAW

———•••———

Cricket: A game invented by religious fundamentalists to explain the idea of eternal hell to non-Christian indigenous peoples of the former British Empire.

JOSEPH O'CONNOR, IRISH NOVELIST

What do they know of cricket
who only cricket know?

C. L. R. JAMES

—— •••• ——

What is human life but
a game of cricket?

3RD DUKE OF DORCHESTER, *LADIES' AND
GENTLEMEN'S MAGAZINE*

—— •••• ——

For when the One Great
Scorer comes
To write against your name,
He marks not that you won or lost
But how you played the game.

GRANTLAND RICE, AMERICAN SPORTS JOURNALIST

EXTRA INNINGS:
ODDBALLS

Remember, linseed
oil for your bat, olive
oil for your lamb.

ALLAN LAMB

Sir, I was horrified to learn the other day that there is now a cricket club in Finland. I left England 25 years ago to get away from people like yourself. Is nowhere sacred?

LETTER TO THE EDITOR OF *THE HELSINKI CRICKETER*

—— •●• ——

I would have died for Yorkshire. I suppose once or twice I nearly did.

BRIAN CLOSE

Sir, Today I learned with interest that the average height of our current Test side is 6 feet. Since there are 11 playing members of the team their total length is therefore 66 feet or 22 yards – the length of the wicket. Is this significant?

MRS PATRICIA CROZIER, LETTER TO *THE TIMES*

I learned that there was a safe
and far-away place on the field
called 'deep' which I always
chose. When 'over' was called,
I simply went more and more
'deep' until I was sitting on the
steps of the pavilions reading
the plays of Noël Coward.

JOHN MORTIMORE, ENGLISH CRICKETER

It's like Manchester United
getting a penalty and Bryan
Robson taking it with his head.

DAVID LLOYD ON THE REVERSE SWEEP

I'll turn the phone off and just watch Ceefax around midday.

GRAEME SWANN, ENGLISH CRICKETER, ON NOT BEING CALLED UP TO PLAY IN THE 2005 ASHES SQUAD

———•••———

I don't think I've actually drunk a beer for 15 years, except a few Guinnesses in Dublin, where it's the law.

IAN BOTHAM

———•••———

Poisoned by his mother? It is good, very good. It ranks up there with 'I got it from the toilet seat'.

DICK POUND, CHAIRMAN OF THE WORLD ANTI-DOPING AGENCY, COMMENTING ON AUSTRALIAN SPIN BOWLER SHANE WARNE'S EXPLANATION THAT HE TESTED POSITIVE FOR A BANNED SUBSTANCE BECAUSE HE HAD TAKEN A DIURETIC GIVEN TO HIM BY HIS MOTHER

Many forget that W. G. Grace was a respected doctor besides being a cricketing legend. One day a timid man turned up at the surgery and asked, 'Is the doctor in?' 'Of course he's in,' snapped the assistant. 'He's been batting since Monday.'

ANONYMOUS

•●•

Let's be getting at them before they get at us.

W. G. GRACE

I suppose going out on your first date is always more exciting than when you've been married for 20 years.

ADAM HOLLIOAKE ON THE CHALLENGE OF CRICKET FOR HIM TOWARDS THE END OF HIS CAREER

———— •●• ————

After the 1776 Revolution, the question of a name for the Chief Executive of the USA was discussed. It was suggested that the word President be used. John Adams thereupon remarked, 'There are Presidents of fire companies and cricket clubs.'

STEPHEN GREEN, SENIOR ECONOMIST, LECTURER AND AUTHOR

Wouldn't it be better if
I got in the fridge?

QASIM OMAR, PAKISTANI BATSMAN, RECEIVING
ICE-PACK TREATMENT FOR BRUISES CAUSED
BY AUSTRALIAN FAST BOWLERS

• ● •

He crossed the line between
eccentricity and idiocy
far too often for someone
who was supposed to be
running English cricket.

IAN BOTHAM ON TED DEXTER

You can't consider yourself a county cricketer until you've eaten half a ton of lettuce.

GARRY SOBERS

———•••———

Ask me for the biggest highlight of my career when I'm lying on my deathbed – then I'll tell you.

IAN BOTHAM

What a magnificent
shot! No, he's out.

TONY GREIG, SOUTH AFRICAN-BORN
COMMENTATOR AND CRICKETER

THE
CRICKET
LOVER'S
COMPANION

Richard Benson

THE CRICKET LOVER'S COMPANION

Richard Benson

£9.99

Hardback

ISBN: 978-1-84953-174-0

I'm confident they play cricket in heaven.
Wouldn't be heaven otherwise, would it?
Patrick Moore

When the umpire has cried 'All out' and you're gearing up for the long walk to the pavilion, prepare to be bowled over by this miscellany of quotes, jokes and trivia on the gentleman's game.

If you're interested in finding out more about our books, find us on Facebook at **Summersdale Publishers** and follow us on Twitter at **@Summersdale**.

www.summersdale.com